vegetarian
main dishes

D1014124

vegetarian
main dishes
from around the world

Chunky Cook Books series
Vegetarian Main Dishes from around the world

First published in the UK in 2004 by
New Internationalist™ Publications Ltd
55 Rectory Road
Oxford OX4 1BW, UK.
www.newint.org
New Internationalist is a registered trade mark.

Cover image: © Claude Sauvageot

Food photography: Caroline Svensson, copyright © Kam & Co, Denmark
Email: studiet@kam.dk
Copyright © all other photographs: individual photographers/agencies.

Design by Alan Hughes/New Internationalist.

Printed in Italy by Amadeus.

Printed on recycled paper.

Reprinted 2005, 2006, 2007, 2008, 2009.

British Library Cataloguing-in-Publication Data.
A catalogue record for this book is available from the British Library.

Library of Congress Cataloguing-in-Publication Data.
A catalogue for this book is available from the Library of Congress.

ISBN 978 1904456 14 8

contents

PORTRAIT PHOTO CREDITS:
DAVID RANSOM/NEW INTERNATIONALIST – PAGE 8
PETER STALKER/NEW INTERNATIONALIST – PAGES 38 & 92
PASCAL MARECHAUX – PAGE 124

introduction

Spicy beans in coconut milk from East Africa, egg-plant/ aubergine casserole from Syria, or a Thai dish – pineapple shell filled with rice, nuts, pineapple chunks and cilantro/coriander – that looks fantastic and tastes delicious. These recipes are easy to prepare and cook. Have a look through and see the great selection of dishes, many accompanied by mouth-watering images from the studio of award-winning Danish photographer Peter Kam.

Cooking is a fun way to relax and try new things, bringing friends and family together. As you eat something from Africa, Latin America or Asia, conversation turns to how people live all over the world. And one of the hot topics today is fair trade – how to ensure that the producers of our food are paid a fair sum for their work.

Fair trade in food and drink items began with one brand of coffee and now includes 130 foods including fruit, juices, vegetables, rice, wine, tea, sugar, honey and nuts. According to the Fair Trade Foundation, this truly is a grassroots movement, growing out of people's awareness that the world price of most foods is *less* than it was 20 years ago. As a result of unfair trade millions of people in the Majority World are struggling to survive.

Worldwide, current annual fair-trade sales amount to over US$950 million. That is only 0.01 per cent of all goods exchanged globally, and includes non-food and drink items such as clothing and crafts. But sales of fairly traded products are increasing rapidly. In the US, Canada and the Pacific Rim, for example, the trade grew by 37 per cent over the past year, according to the 2003 Report on Fair Trade Trends, with sales reaching $250 million. Europe's market is more than twice as big, and grew by one third last year.

Switzerland heads the list of European countries buying fair trade goods, with Britain in second place. In the UK fair trade food sales have hit $165 million per year, after growth of between 40 and 90 per cent each year for a decade, according to *The Guardian* newspaper.

Of course the supermarkets are quick to spot a trend and are stocking their shelves with fair trade and organic items. The Co-op was the first in Britain to take fair trade food seriously after consulting shoppers, in 1995. One in four of its bananas and chocolate bars are now fairly traded. People are prepared to pay a little more as a premium in order to give a guaranteed price to the producers.

See more about fair trade on page 170, and try using some fair trade and organic products for these recipes. ∎

africa

maharagwe <small>serves **4-6**</small>

spiced beans in coconut milk

1 onion, chopped

1 cup / 225 g black-eyed, pinto or rosecoco beans, cooked

3 tomatoes, chopped

1$^1/_2$ teaspoons turmeric

1 teaspoon chili powder

1 tablespoon fresh cilantro/coriander leaves or parsley, chopped

1$^1/_2$ cups / 360 ml coconut milk

oil

salt

1 Using a deep, heavy pan, heat the oil and cook the onion gently until soft and golden.

2 Partially mash the beans with a fork and then spoon them into the onion. Add the chopped tomatoes and mix well.

3 Now put in the turmeric and chili powder, seasoning and half the cilantro/coriander leaves. After that, pour in the coconut milk, stirring to blend the ingredients.

4 Cover the pan and leave it to simmer for 10 minutes before garnishing with the remaining cilantro/coriander leaves or parsley. Serve with rice.

bean curry

serves **4**

black-eyed beans

1 cup / 225 g beans, cooked	1 teaspoon turmeric
1 onion, chopped	1 teaspoon ground coriander
3 cloves garlic, crushed	1 cup / 240 ml coconut milk
1/2 green chili, chopped finely	oil
1 teaspoon fresh ginger, grated	salt

1 First sauté the onion in hot oil and then add the garlic, chili, and ginger. Stir these ingredients and cook for 3-5 minutes.

2 Next put in the turmeric and ground coriander and cook these for about 30 seconds.

3 Now spoon in the cooked beans and mix them into the flavorings, crushing them a little. When this is done, pour in the coconut milk, stirring as you do so. Season, cover and simmer at a low heat for 30-40 minutes or until the curry is moist but thick.

shiro wat

serves **2**

peanut stew

2 cups / 250 g peanuts*, ground or 1 cup / 225 g peanut butter

4 tablespoons / 50 g margarine

1 small onion, chopped

1 tablespoon tomato paste

1/2 teaspoon fresh or dried thyme

1/2 teaspoon ground mixed spice or a mixture of ground cinnamon and nutmeg

1 teaspoon paprika

2 1/2 cups / 590 ml water

salt and pepper

*If using peanuts, measure them first and then grind them.

1 To start making the stew, heat the margarine in a pan and cook the onion for about 3 minutes until it begins to turn golden. Then add the tomato paste, thyme, mixed spice and paprika, salt and pepper. Stir well to combine the ingredients.

2 When the onion is cooked, put in the finely ground peanuts or peanut butter and enough of the water to make a smooth but thick sauce. Stir constantly while you add the liquid.

3 Check the seasoning and then let the stew heat through before serving with millet, bulghur or rice and a cucumber salad.

ETHIOPIA

yemesirkik

serves **4-6**

lentil wat/stew

1 onion, chopped

2-3 teaspoons berberé paste*

2 cloves garlic, crushed

2 cups / 450 g brown or red lentils, cooked

water

oil

salt

*Hot pepper paste available in specialist stores.

1 Heat 1 tablespoon of oil in a heavy pan and sauté the onion. When it is soft and turning golden, add the berberé paste and garlic and mix well.

2 Cook for a minute or two and then add a little water and 2 more tablespoons of oil.

3 Mash the cooked lentils and put these into the onion mix; stir often so that the mixture does not burn.

4 Now pour in a little more water and sprinkle in salt to taste. Cook for 5-10 minutes longer to let the flavors expand and then set aside to cool. Serve warm or cool with funkaso, pittas or chapatis.

GHANA

bean stew

serves **4**

with black-eyed beans

**1 cup / 225 g
black-eyed beans,
cooked**

1 onion, sliced

2 tomatoes, chopped

**1/2 chili, chopped or 1/2
teaspoon chili powder**

**1-2 tablespoons
red palm oil***

salt and pepper

*If you cannot find this,
use margarine or cooking oil.

1 Mash the cooked beans and set aside. Heat the oil in a pan and cook the onion and tomatoes a little before adding the mashed beans, chili and seasoning.

2 Let the mixture cook for 10 minutes or so until it combines well. Stir from time to time and add a little water if it becomes too dry. Serve hot with mashed yams, fried plantains or rice.

aprapransa
serves **4**

palm nut stew

1 onion, chopped

1 cup / 225 g black-eyed beans, cooked

2-4 tablespoons palm butter or peanut butter*

2 tomatoes, chopped

2 tomatoes, sliced

3 tablespoons corn/maize flour, toasted†

1 tablespoon red palm or cooking oil*

1 tablespoon lemon juice

water

salt and pepper

*Canned palm butter or palm nut pulp is available in specialist food stores. Peanut butter makes an acceptable alternative.

†To toast the flour, spread it out in a heavy shallow pan and cook it, dry, over a gentle heat until it turns golden.

1 Heat the palm oil in a heavy pan and cook the onion until it is soft. Then add the cooked beans and the palm or peanut butter and a little water as necessary and cook for 5 minutes.

2 Now put in the chopped tomatoes, salt and pepper. Cook for another 5 minutes before tipping in the toasted corn/maize flour; stir well.

3 Pour in the lemon juice, add more water or seasoning if desired and simmer the pot very gently for a further 15 minutes before serving, topped with the tomato slices.

KENYA

dengu

serves **4**

green gram/mung beans in coconut milk

1 cup / 225 g mung dal, cooked*

1 onion, sliced

³/₄ cup / 200 ml coconut milk

¹/₄ teaspoon paprika

slices of red bell pepper

oil

salt

*Mung dal are the hulled, split form of mung beans.

1 Sprinkle salt to taste on the cooked dal and partially mash with a fork; set aside.

2 Now heat the oil in a heavy pan and sauté the onion till soft. When it is ready, gradually pour in the coconut milk. Bring the mixture slowly to the boil, stirring well.

3 Next put in the dal and stir so that the ingredients and flavors mingle. Add the paprika and check the seasoning. Garnish with some slices of red bell pepper and serve with rice or mashed sweet potatoes.

KENYA

nyoyo

serves **4-6**

beans and corn

1 onion, chopped

3 red bell peppers, chopped

4 tomatoes, sliced

1 cup / 225 g black-eyed beans, cooked

2 cups / 300 g corn kernels, cooked or use canned sweetcorn, drained

1 teaspoon paprika

oil

salt and pepper

1 Start by heating the oil in a pan and cooking the onion until it is soft. Then put in the bell peppers and, a little later, the tomatoes.

2 While that is cooking, combine the cooked beans and corn in a bowl and add salt to taste.

3 Now put the corn and bean mixture into the pan containing the onion and tomatoes and season with pepper.

4 Mix well, cover the pot and cook for about 15 minutes or until the ingredients have blended together. Add more water if required during the cooking as the dish should be moist. Serve with rice or bulghur/ cracked wheat and a green vegetable or salad.

irio

serves **6**

maize/corn and bean mash

3 cups / 450 g corn kernels, cooked

1 cup / 200 g haricot, sugar or red kidney beans, soaked and cooked

$^1/_2$ pound / 225 g potatoes, chopped

2$^1/_2$ cups / 590 ml stock or water

1 pound / 450 g pumpkin leaves or spinach, chopped

salt and pepper

1 First boil the potatoes in the stock or water for 10 minutes or until they are almost cooked. Then add in the beans, corn kernels and the spinach or pumpkin leaves.

2 Continue to cook together until the potatoes are ready, the beans and corn hot and the spinach or pumpkin leaves are cooked.

3 Then drain off most of the liquid into a bowl and keep it. Add a little margarine, salt and pepper to the bean and potato mix and mash well using a fork or a potato masher. Put in more liquid if required to make the consistency you prefer and then serve hot.

KENYA

serves **4**

casserole

with sweet potatoes, cheese and onion

1 pound / 450 g sweet potatoes, peeled and sliced thinly

a little water or stock

1 tablespoon margarine

1 large onion, sliced thinly into circles

1 cup / 225 g cheese, grated

1/2 teaspoon chili powder

salt and pepper

Heat oven to 350°F/180°C/Gas 4

1 Grease an oven-proof dish and line it with the sweet potato slices. Pour in just enough water or stock to coat the base of the dish evenly and then dot margarine amongst the layers of potato.

2 Arrange the onion circles on top of the sweet potato and finish up with the cheese. Sprinkle on the chili powder, salt and pepper.

3 Cover the dish and cook for 1 hour, removing the lid for the last 15 minutes to brown. Serve hot with salad.

wake-ewa

serves **4-6**

black-eyed beans with sauce

2 cups / 450 g
black-eyed beans,
soaked and cooked

1 large onion

4 tablespoons oil

1 teaspoon chili powder

1 teaspoon
ground coriander

1 teaspoon thyme

3 tomatoes,
chopped finely

1 teaspoon sugar

salt

1 First cut the onion in half. Grate one half and then slice the rest finely.

2 Warm the oil in a pan and soften the onion slices in it.

3 Meanwhile combine the grated onion, chili, coriander and thyme in a bowl with the tomatoes and add this to the cooked onion slices. Continue to cook the mixture gently for 10-15 minutes, stirring constantly.

4 After this put in the beans, mash them a little with a fork and then add the sugar and salt. Mix everything well and cook for 5-10 minutes to heat all the ingredients before serving with salad and rice or fufu.

vegetable stew

serves **6-8**

3-4 tablespoons peanut oil

2 large onions, finely chopped

1 chili, chopped or 1 teaspoon chili powder or 1 teaspoon ground ginger

1 pound / 450 g potatoes, quartered

1 small turnip, chopped coarsely

2 large carrots, sliced

1 cup / 150 g pumpkin, squash or marrow, peeled and cubed

1 cup / 240 ml water

1 cup / 240 ml tomato paste

$^1/_2$ pound / 225 g cabbage, chopped

1 cup / 225 g leafy greens (such as pumpkin leaves/spinach)

2 large tomatoes, quartered

1 cup / 225 g peanut butter

salt and pepper

1 Firstly heat the oil in a large pan or stew pot and then brown the onions, adding the chili or ginger when the onions are soft. Cook for 2-3 minutes.

2 Next put in the potatoes and turnip pieces and cook them for 10 minutes before adding the carrots and pumpkin. Continue cooking for a further 10 minutes.

3 Now pour the water onto the tomato paste, stirring as you do so and then add this to the vegetable pot. Cover, bring to the boil and then reduce the heat and simmer until the vegetables are nearly done.

4 At this point add the cabbage, the other leafy vegetables and the tomatoes. Season with salt and pepper.

5 When cooked, remove about $^{1}/_{2}$ cup/120 ml of the broth and mix it with the peanut butter to make a smooth paste. Put this back into the pot and stir; simmer for another 10 minutes. Serve with rice or corn/maize porridge.

bredie

serves **2-4**

bean and tomato stew

2 onions, chopped

2 cloves garlic, chopped

1 tablespoon shallots, leek or chives, chopped

1 teaspoon fresh ginger, grated

2 cardamoms

1 teaspoon fennel seed

pinch of chili powder

1 teaspoon ground coriander

$^1/_2$ cup / 110 g rosecoco, pinto or sugar beans, cooked

1 pound / 450 g tomatoes, chopped

$^1/_2$ pound / 225 g potatoes, cut into large pieces

1 bayleaf

handful fennel leaves

1 teaspoon thyme, marjoram and/or oregano

1 teaspoon sugar

$^1/_2$ glass / 75 ml red wine

$^1/_2$ cup / 50 g raisins, sultanas, dried apricots or other fruit

a little stock or water

oil

salt and pepper

1 Sauté the onions in the hot oil for a few minutes and when they have begun to soften put in the garlic, shallots, ginger, cardamoms, fennel seed, chili and coriander. Cook for 10 minutes or so, stirring frequently.

2 Now add the beans, tomatoes, potatoes, bayleaf, fennel leaves, thyme, marjoram, oregano, sugar, wine and the raisins or dried fruit. Season, cover the pot and cook very gently for $1^1/_2$ hours, adding some stock or water as desired, and stirring occasionally.

coconut & bean stew

serves **4**

3 cloves garlic, crushed

1 green chili, finely chopped or 1 teaspoon chili powder

1 tablespoon ground cumin

1 tablespoon ground coriander

2 teaspoons turmeric

1 tablespoon fresh cilantro/coriander leaves, chopped

1 cup / 75 g dried/ desiccated coconut

1 cup / 225 g pinto, rosecoco or black-eyed beans, cooked

1 cup / 175 g potatoes, diced and parboiled

lime or lemon juice to taste

2 tablespoons coconut or other oil

salt

1 Heat the oil and sizzle the garlic together with the chili or chili powder for half a minute.

2 When this is ready, put in the cumin, coriander, turmeric and the cilantro/coriander leaves. Cook for a minute or two, stirring them round to blend. Add the coconut and mix this in too.

3 Now bring in the beans and potatoes; season and then pour the lime or lemon juice over. Cook for 10 minutes or so until everything is blended together and then serve with green vegetables.

asia

labra

serves **4**

mixed spicy vegetables

1/2 teaspoon turmeric

1/2 pound / 225 g
potatoes, chopped into
small cubes

1/2 cup / 110 g
cauliflower, cut into
small pieces

1 teaspoon
panch phoron*

1/2 teaspoon
fresh ginger,
grated

1 cup / 110 g snowpeas/
mangetout, sliced into 2
or 3 pieces

1/2 egg-plant/aubergine,
cut into small cubes

1 plantain/savory banana,
sliced

oil

salt

*Panch phoron or five mixed
spices is made up of cumin, fennel, bayleaf, fenugreek and onion
seeds. You can buy it ready mixed
from Asian stores, or else purchase
the individual spices to make your
own mix.

1 Taking a heavy pan, heat the oil and sprinkle in the turmeric and salt. Cook them for a few moments and then add the diced potatoes, stirring them into the turmeric mix.

2 After 5 minutes, put in the cauliflower and stir-fry it with the potatoes for another 3 minutes or so, until they are partially cooked and then remove them from the pan and set aside.

3 Now pouring in more oil as necessary, scatter in the panch phoron and let it sizzle until the spices turn brown but do not burn. Then put in the ginger and cook for 1 minute.

4 Next put in the snowpeas/ mangetout, egg-plant/ aubergine and banana and sauté for 3 minutes before returning the cauliflower and potatoes to the pan.

5 Stir-fry all the ingredients for several minutes and then cover the pan and let it cook slowly for up to 20 minutes or until the potatoes are soft. Season, and stir from time to time. Serve with rice or chapatis.

spicy stir-fry

serves **4**

$^1/_2$ teaspoon turmeric

$^1/_2$ pound / 225 g
potatoes, chopped into
small cubes

1 onion, finely chopped

1 bayleaf

$^1/_2$ teaspoon ground
cumin

$^1/_2$ teaspoon
ground ginger

$^1/_4$ teaspoon chili powder

4 tomatoes, chopped

1 cup / 110 g white
cabbage, finely sliced

$^1/_2$ cup / 85 g peas

oil

salt

1 Start by heating the oil in a heavy pan and put in the turmeric and some salt. Fry for a few seconds and then add the cubed potatoes, turning frequently so that they turn yellow from the turmeric. Cook them for 5-10 minutes (they will complete their cooking later) and then remove them from the oil and set aside.

2 Adding more oil if necessary, now sauté the onion slices until they are soft and transparent. Then add the bayleaf, cumin, ginger and chili powder.

3 Stir well and put in the tomatoes. When they have begun to break down, add the cabbage bit by bit, stirring it in well so that it is sautéed in the spices. Cover and cook gently for 3-5 minutes.

4 Finally, put in the peas and semi-fried potatoes and seasoning. Mix well, replace the cover and continue to cook for 5-10 minutes or until the potatoes are ready.

CAMBODIA

stir-fry

serves **4-6**

with noodles

1 onion, finely sliced

1¹/₂ red chilis, chopped

1 teaspoon fresh ginger, finely chopped

2 cups / 100 g chinese or ordinary mushrooms, sliced

¹/₂ pound / 225 g egg noodles

2 carrots, finely sliced

1 cup / 150 g broccoli or cauliflower, chopped

1 cup / 110 g snowpeas/ mangetout, cut in half

soy sauce

1-2 tablespoons fresh cilantro/coriander leaves, chopped

oil

1 Prepare the noodles by plunging them into boiling water and then remove the pan from the heat and set aside for 6 minutes, or cook according to the packet instructions. Keep hot.

2 Then heat the oil in the wok and sauté the onion gently for a few minutes until it begins to soften. Put in the chilis and the ginger now and stir-fry these for 2 minutes before adding the mushrooms. These should also be sautéed for 2-3 minutes; then reduce the heat.

3 While that is happening, boil some water in a separate saucepan and cook the carrots, broccoli or cauliflower and snowpeas/mangetout for 3 minutes; drain and then add to the onion mixture. Stir fry for 2-3 minutes, sprinkle on soy sauce to taste, and mix everything well.

4 When they are ready, drain the noodles and scoop them onto a large serving dish. Pile the stir-fry on top, scatter the cilantro/coriander leaves over and serve at once, with additional soy sauce if required.

stir-fry

serves **4**

gingered vegetables

1 pound / 450 g mixed vegetables, sliced finely*

1/2 pound / 225 g chinese cabbage, sliced

2 teaspoons fresh ginger, grated

2 cloves garlic, crushed

1 point star anise, crushed or 1/2 teaspoon aniseed, crushed

2 tablespoons soy sauce

1 teaspoon cornstarch mixed to a paste with 1 tablespoon water

1/2 cup / 120 ml hot water

oil

salt

*Such as leeks, cauliflower, green beans, peas, scallions/spring onions and carrots.

1 In a wok or pan, heat the oil and then fry the ginger with the garlic for 30 seconds. Add the star anise or aniseed and stir for a further 30 seconds.

2 Next, put in the mixed vegetables, stir-frying briskly for 1 minute. When they have begun to soften, add the cabbage.

3 Lower the heat to a gentle simmer and meanwhile, taking a small bowl, mix the soy sauce with the hot water and salt.

4 Now pour this mixture into the vegetables, stir and then cover the pan or wok and simmer for 4 minutes.

5 After that, sweep the vegetables to one side of the pan and spoon the cornstarch mix into the center. Stir until it thickens and then quickly toss the vegetables in it and serve at once.

omelet

serves **2**

with bean sprouts

3 eggs

1 tablespoon milk

dash of soy sauce

2 cups / 100 g bean
sprouts

3 scallions / spring
onions, chopped finely

1 tablespoon oil

salt and pepper

1 In a bowl, beat the eggs and then mix in the milk, soy sauce, salt and pepper, scallions/spring onions and the bean sprouts.

2 When this is done, heat the oil in a pan, pour in the egg mixture and cook quickly, turning once. Serve right away.

dal

serves **2**

with tomatoes

1 cup / 225 g red lentils

2 small potatoes, diced

2 tablespoons oil or ghee

1 large onion, chopped

1-2 cloves garlic, crushed

1/2 green bell pepper, chopped

1 teaspoon ground cumin

1 teaspoon turmeric

1 teaspoon madras (hot) curry powder

2 teaspoons ground ginger

1 can chopped tomatoes

salt and pepper

TO SERVE:

1 banana, sliced

mango chutney

cucumber raita

1 Place the lentils and potatoes into a pan of boiling water and cook them for about 10 minutes. Drain.

2 Next heat the oil or ghee in a pan and add the onion, garlic and bell pepper. Cook these until they are soft and then put in the cumin, turmeric, curry powder, ginger, salt and pepper. Continue to cook for 1-2 minutes before adding the tomatoes.

3 After this, let the mixture cook for a further minute or so and then put in the lentils and potatoes. Simmer gently for 5-10 minutes until everything is soft and hot. Serve with rice and side dishes such as cucumber raita as desired.

vegetable curry

serves **4**

4 tablespoons / 50 g margarine or ghee

1 onion, sliced

1-2 cloves garlic, crushed

1 tablespoon curry powder

1 green bell pepper, chopped

$2^1/_4$ cups / 350 g vegetables, diced and parboiled*

1 tablespoon desiccated coconut

a little water or stock

$^1/_2$ teaspoon turmeric

salt and pepper

*Such as potatoes, carrots, zucchini/courgettes, peas and okra – or whatever you have to hand.

1 First of all, melt the margarine or ghee in a large pan and cook the onion and garlic until they are lightly browned. Sprinkle in the curry powder and turmeric; cook for 2 minutes, stirring frequently.

2 Put in the bell pepper and let it cook for a few minutes before adding the other vegetables, coconut and enough water or stock to cover the base of the pan and prevent sticking.

3 Now cover and simmer until the vegetables are tender, adding more water or stock if the mixture looks too dry. Season with pepper and salt and serve with rice, chutney and yogurt.

serves **4**

chickpea curry

with tomatoes

1¹/₂ cups / 225 g chickpeas, soaked and cooked

2 small papayas/paw-paw, cubed or use canned (drained and rinsed)

2 medium onions, sliced

1 green chili, chopped

2 tablespoons / 50 g margarine or ghee

¹/₂ teaspoon ground cumin

¹/₂ teaspoon garam masala

3 tablespoons / 75 g desiccated coconut

salt and pepper

1 To make the curry, melt the margarine or ghee in a saucepan and sauté the onions until they are golden.

2 Then add the chili, cumin, garam masala, salt and pepper and cook for 1 minute, stirring well. After this, put in the coconut and add enough water to make a little sauce. Simmer for about 5 minutes or until the sauce thickens.

3 Add the chickpeas and heat them through. Then put in the papaya/paw-paw pieces and cook gently for 2 minutes before serving with plain boiled rice or chapatis.

mushroom curry

serves **4**

1 pound / 450 g
mushrooms, sliced

1 onion, sliced

3 cloves garlic, sliced

2-4 tomatoes, chopped

$1/4$ teaspoon ground
ginger

1 teaspoon chili powder

$1/2$ teaspoon ground
cumin

seeds from 3
cardamoms, crushed

1 teaspoon garam
masala

1 tablespoon fresh
cilantro/coriander
leaves, chopped

$1/2$ cup / 120 ml tomato
juice or water

oil or ghee

salt

1 Start by heating the fat and cooking the onion until it is translucent. Then put in the garlic followed by the mushrooms and sauté these until they begin to soften.

2 After that, add the tomatoes, ginger, chili powder, cumin, cardamoms and garam masala, the cilantro/coriander leaves and salt. Stir these in well.

3 Now pour in the water or juice and cook gently for 20-30 minutes until the mushrooms are very soft. Serve with rice or chapatis.

avial

serves **2-4**

vegetables in coconut milk

4 drumsticks, chopped*

1 cup / 175 g yam or sweet potato, diced

1/2 cup / 80 g plantain (green banana), chopped

1/2 cup / 60 g ladies' fingers/okras, chopped

1/2 cup / 60 g peas

1/2 teaspoon turmeric

1/2 fresh green chili, sliced

1/2 teaspoon cumin seeds

1/2 teaspoon ground cumin

5 curry leaves

1/2 cup / 120 ml yogurt

3/4 cup / 200 ml coconut milk

oil

salt and pepper

*Drumsticks (long, thin, ridged green pods) are available in some Indian stores. Or use 1/2 pound/250 g spinach.

1 Heat up a little water and mix in the turmeric powder. When it boils add the drumsticks, yam or sweet potato and plantain and cook for 10 minutes.

2 Now add the ladies' fingers/okras and peas and continue to cook for a further 10-20 minutes. Drain, retaining the water.

3 While that is cooking, grind the sliced chili with the cumin seeds adding a little coconut milk to make a paste.

4 Heat some oil in a pan and stir in the drained vegetables. Add the spice paste, yogurt, coconut milk and curry leaves. Season.

5 Cook very gently, stirring regularly so that it does not catch, until the ingredients have combined. If it seems too dry, or if you prefer a more liquid mixture, add some of the retained cooking water or more coconut milk.

biryani

serves **6**

spiced vegetable rice

1 pound / 450 g rice

$1/2$ pound / 225 g mixed frozen or fresh peas and chopped carrots

6 cloves garlic, crushed

$1 1/2$ teaspoons ground ginger

4 cloves

1 teaspoon poppy seeds, crushed

1 black or 3 green cardamoms

$1/2$ cinnamon stick

2 bayleaves

1 onion, sliced finely

$2 1/2$ cups / 590 ml water

oil

salt

1 Soak the rice for 30 minutes, in enough water to cover, then drain.

2 Mash the garlic and ginger together with 1 tablespoon of water to make a paste.

3 In a heavy pan, heat the oil and when it is hot add the cloves, poppy seeds, cardamoms, cinnamon and bayleaves; stir.

4 Now put in the onion and sauté until it is transparent. Then the garlic and ginger paste can go in. Stir and fry for 30 seconds.

5 When this is done, begin to add the mixed vegetables. Start with the harder ones such as carrots and stir-fry these for 1 minute before putting in the others.

6 The drained rice goes in next, together with the salt. Mix all the ingredients and then continue to cook over a low heat for 3-4 minutes.

7 Now pour in the water, cover and bring to the boil. Then turn down the heat to allow a gentle simmer and cook for 25 minutes. Serve with yogurt and tomato.

caldin

serves **4-6**

coconut curry

**¹/₂ pound / 225 g
potatoes, diced**

**¹/₂ pound / 225 g
cauliflower, chopped**

1 onion, sliced

**¹/₂ teaspoon fresh ginger,
grated**

2 cloves garlic, crushed

**¹/₂ teaspoon black
pepper**

**¹/₂ teaspoon
ground cumin**

**1 teaspoon ground
coriander**

1 teaspoon turmeric

1 teaspoon sugar

**1 green chili,
chopped finely**

**2 tablespoons
coconut milk**

1 tablespoon vinegar

2 cups / 480 ml water

**¹/₂ tablespoon
tamarind paste**

salt

oil

1 Take a large pan or wok and heat the oil in it. Then fry the onion until it turns golden brown.

2 Now reduce the heat and gradually add the ginger, garlic, pepper, cumin, coriander, turmeric, sugar and chili.

3 Mix these in well and then spoon in the coconut milk followed by the vinegar.

4 Pour on the water and add the tamarind paste. Then, turning up the heat, bring the pan to the boil. At this stage put in the vegetables. Simmer the ingredients until everything is cooked and then serve with chapatis or rice.

INDIA

dal

serves **4**

with coconut

1 cup / 225 g red lentils*

2¹/₂ cups / 590 ml water

¹/₂ teaspoon turmeric

1 teaspoon fresh ginger, chopped coarsely

¹/₂ onion, chopped

3 tablespoons dried/desiccated coconut

1 tablespoon margarine

salt

*If using dal other than red lentils, soak them first for 15 minutes and then cook them until they are just ready.

1 Put the lentils or other dal in a pan and add the water. Bring to the boil, and remove any froth that rises to the surface.

2 Now add the turmeric, ginger, onion and salt and simmer together for 10 minutes or until the dal is almost done. The water should be almost completely absorbed. Season.

3 At this point, melt the margarine in another pan and stir in the coconut. Cook it gently, stirring, until the coconut turns a rich brown color.

4 When the dal is ready, spoon it into a serving dish and sprinkle the hot coconut over it.

chhloe

serves **4**

chickpeas with tomatoes

2 onions, thinly sliced

4 cloves garlic, crushed

**1-2 green chilis,
finely sliced**

1 teaspoon turmeric

1 teaspoon paprika

**1 tablespoon ground
cumin**

**1 tablespoon ground
coriander**

1 teaspoon garam masala

4 tomatoes, chopped

**2 tablespoons fresh
cilantro/coriander leaves,
chopped**

**2 tablespoons fresh mint,
chopped or 2 teaspoons
dried**

**1¼ cups / 225 g
chickpeas, cooked**

oil or ghee

salt and pepper

1 Take a heavy pan and heat the oil or ghee. When it is hot, put in the onions and garlic and sauté them gently for about 5 minutes until golden.

2 Now add the chilis, turmeric, paprika, cumin, ground coriander and garam masala and fry for 2 minutes, stirring frequently.

3 When this is done, put in the tomatoes, 1 tablespoon of the fresh cilantro/coriander leaves together with the mint and cook, stirring, for about 10 minutes until the tomatoes have mushed down to a purée.

4 Put in the chickpeas now and cook for a further 10-15 minutes or better still, remove the pot from the heat and leave for several hours so that the flavors blend well. Then re-heat, scattering the remaining chopped cilantro/coriander leaves on top. Serve with yogurt and cucumber raita or sambal.

shabnam kari

serves **2-3**

curry with peas and mushrooms

³/₄ cup / 110 g frozen or fresh peas

1 onion, finely sliced

2 cloves

1 tablespoon raisins or sultanas

2 cups / 100 g mushrooms, sliced

3 tablespoons cream⁺

4 tablespoons yogurt

¹/₂ cup / 120 ml water

2 tablespoons ghee or margarine

handful whole or chopped cashew nuts⁺

salt

FOR THE PASTE

5 cloves, stalks discarded

¹/₂ teaspoon fresh ginger, grated

2 tablespoons cashew nuts, chopped

2 tablespoons poppy seeds

seeds from 2 cardamom pods

1 green chili, finely chopped

salt

⁺optional ingredients

1 Boil the peas for a few minutes in a little water until they are just tender, then drain them and set aside.

2 While they are cooking, prepare the paste. Put the cloves, ginger, cashew nuts, poppy seeds, cardamom seeds and chili into a blender, adding some water as necessary to give a smooth consistency. Set aside.

3 Returning to the main ingredients, heat the ghee or margarine and sauté the onion until it is soft and golden. Add the cloves and cook for a few moments before spooning in the blended paste, together with the raisins or sultanas. Stir the mixture round while it cooks for 2-3 minutes.

4 After this, add the peas, mushrooms, cream, yogurt and water. Stir well to amalgamate and season with salt. Cook gently for 5 minutes before serving with the cashew nuts scattered on top.

tamarind dal serves 2-4

1 tablespoon / 50 g tamarind pulp, soaked in 1/2 cup / 120 ml warm water for 20 minutes

1 teaspoon cumin seeds

1 green chili, chopped

1 teaspoon fresh ginger, finely chopped

1/2 teaspoon chili powder

2 teaspoons garam masala

2 tablespoons fresh cilantro/coriander leaves, chopped

1/2 cup / 110 g red lentils, cooked

oil

salt

1 When the tamarind has soaked place it in a sieve above the bowl containing the water it was soaked in and press the pulp through. Mix well with the water and set aside.

2 Heat a pan without oil and then toast the cumin seeds in it, stirring frequently until they turn a darker color. Then transfer them to a bowl or mortar and crush them.

3 Now add the chili, ginger, chili powder, garam masala, cumin seeds, cilantro/coriander leaves and a little salt to the bowl containing the tamarind water. Stir well and leave to stand for 15 minutes.

4 While that is happening, heat up some oil in a pan and fry the lentils over a brisk heat for 5 minutes. After that, pour in the tamarind mixture and continue to simmer for 5-10 minutes, stirring to distribute the spicy sauce. Serve with rice or phulkas.

dhansak

serves **4**

lentil purée

1 teaspoon cumin seeds

1 teaspoon mustard seeds

1 stick cinnamon

6 green cardamom pods

1 onion, finely chopped

2 cloves garlic, crushed

1 carrot, thinly sliced

3-4 tomatoes, chopped

1 red or green bell pepper, chopped

1 cup / 225 g toor dal or red lentils, cooked

1 tablespoon mild curry powder

1/2 cup / 120 ml coconut milk

4 tablespoons fresh cilantro/coriander leaves, chopped

2 tablespoons fresh mint, chopped or 2 teaspoons dried

1 cup / 150 g paneer cheese, cubed and fried*

2 tablespoons cashew nuts

a squeeze of lemon juice

oil

salt

*This curd cheese (obtainable in Asian stores) is rather similar to bean-curd/tofu in that it absorbs surrounding aromas while providing protein. You can omit it and serve the dish with yogurt instead.

1 First heat the oil in a wok or large pan and then put in the cumin seeds, mustard seeds, cinnamon and cardamoms. Stir-fry them for a few moments before adding the onion, garlic and carrot. Then cook these, stirring all the time, for 3-4 minutes.

2 Next add the tomatoes and bell pepper and simmer for 10 minutes. When this is done, spoon in the lentils. Mix in the curry powder, coconut milk, cilantro/coriander leaves, mint and salt.

3 Stir well to combine all the ingredients and then add the paneer, if using, as well as the cashew nuts. Squeeze in some lemon juice to taste and continue to cook gently for a further 10 minutes, stirring so that it does not stick. Add a little water or more coconut milk if necessary.

sayur lodeh

serves **4**

vegetables in coconut milk

¹/₂ pound / 225 g potatoes, diced

1 carrot, chopped

¹/₂ cup / 75 g green beans, sliced

1 cup / 100 g cabbage, shredded

1 cup / 50 g beansprouts

2 onions, sliced

2 cloves garlic, crushed

¹/₂ cup / 50 g cucumber, sliced

1 teaspoon tamarind paste, crumbled

¹/₂ teaspoon fresh ginger, grated

2 teaspoons ground coriander

1¹/₂ cups / 360 ml coconut milk

oil

salt

1 Boil some water and cook the potatoes and carrot for 5 minutes. Then add the green beans and cabbage and cook for a further 3 minutes. Drain, retaining the water, and set aside.

2 Boil the water again, remove the pan from the heat and put in the beansprouts to soak for 2 minutes. Drain.

3 Now heat the oil in a wok and fry the onions until they are soft. Next, put in the garlic and then add the sliced cucumber, cooking these for 3-5 minutes.

4 Mix the tamarind paste with the ginger, coriander, coconut milk and salt.

5 Pour the coconut milk mixture over the cucumber and onion. Simmer gently for about 5 minutes.

6 Stir, and then put in the potatoes, carrot, cabbage and beansprouts. Season, and simmer again, stirring.

gado-gado

serves **4**

vegetable salad with peanut sauce

THE SALAD	THE SAUCE
2 carrots, finely sliced	1 tablespoon oil
2 medium potatoes, sliced	1-2 cloves garlic, crushed
1 cup / 150 g shredded cabbage	1 small onion, grated
2 cups / 100 g bean sprouts	1 green chili, finely chopped or 1 teaspoon chili powder
1 tablespoon oil	$1/2$ cup / 110 g crunchy peanut butter
1 cup / 150 g bean-curd/ tofu, cut in 1 inch / 2.5 cm cubes	1 teaspoon lemon juice or vinegar
1 cup / 100 g sliced cucumber	$1/2$ cup / 50 g creamed coconut melted in $1/2$ cup/120 ml hot water
2 medium tomatoes, sliced	salt
2 hard-boiled eggs, sliced	
1 scallion/spring onion, sliced	

1 Steam or parboil the carrots and potato slices for 5 minutes. Then cook the cabbage, bean sprouts and cucumber for 1-2 minutes. Drain the vegetables and leave them to cool.

2 If using bean-curd/tofu, heat 1 tablespoon of oil in a wok or pan and cook it for 3-5 minutes, turning from time to time so that it is golden all over.

3 Now arrange the steamed vegetables in layers on a flat dish or plate starting with the cabbage, then the potato slices, then bean sprouts, carrots and cucumber. Put the tomatoes, sliced eggs and tofu on top.

4 For the sauce, heat the oil in a wok or large pan. Stir-fry the garlic, onion and chili for 2-3 minutes.

5 Add the peanut butter, lemon juice or vinegar and coconut milk and simmer for 2-3 minutes. The sauce should be thick but pourable, so add more lemon juice and/or milk if necessary.

6 To serve, pour the hot sauce over the vegetables and garnish with the scallion/ spring onion slices.

tauhu goreng serves 4

filled bean-curd/tofu cakes

4 bean-curd/tofu cakes

1 cup / 50 g bean sprouts, scalded

3 inches / 7.5 cms cucumber, shredded

salt

oil

FOR THE SAUCE

2 green chilis, sliced

2 red chilis, sliced

2 cloves garlic, crushed

1¹/₂ tablespoons soy sauce

1¹/₂ tablespoons vinegar

2 cups / 225 g peanuts, roasted and blended*

³/₄ cup / 200 ml water

2 tablespoons chopped cilantro/coriander leaves

salt

*Or use ¹/₂ cup / 110 g peanut butter.

1 Heat enough oil (about 2 inches/5 cms deep) in a wok or pan to deep-fry the bean-curd/tofu cakes until they are slightly brown. Lift them out and let them cool.

2 Then cut each cake into 2 pieces and make a deep slit across the center to form a pocket.

3 After that, mix the bean sprouts and cucumber in a bowl and season well before filling the bean-curd/tofu pouches.

4 For the sauce, pound or blend the chilis and garlic together. Then add the soy sauce, vinegar and salt. Next put in the ground peanuts and add the water a little at a time. Stir to make a smooth coating sauce.

5 Arrange the stuffed bean-curd/tofu cakes on a dish; garnish with slices of cucumber and fresh cilantro/coriander leaves and serve the peanut sauce separately.

dal-bhaat & tarkari

serves **4**

lentils and curried vegetables

FOR THE DAL

1 onion, chopped

2 cloves garlic, crushed

$1/4$ teaspoon fresh ginger, grated

$1/2$ teaspoon turmeric

1 cup / 225 g red lentils

oil

salt

FOR THE CURRIED VEGETABLES

1 pound / 450 g mixed vegetables, chopped (potatoes, carrots, peas)

$1/2$ green chili, finely chopped or $1/2$ teaspoon chili powder

$1/4$ teaspoon fresh ginger, grated

1 teaspoon ground coriander

1 teaspoon ground cumin

oil

salt

1 For the dal, heat up some oil in a saucepan and then sauté the onion for a few minutes followed by the garlic until both ingredients are soft but not browned. Now add the ginger and cook this too for a minute or so.

2 Next, put in the lentils and the turmeric and stir them round so that they combine with the onion, garlic and ginger.

3 When this is done, pour on enough water to submerge the lentils, cover the pot, and bring to the boil. Then reduce the heat and simmer for about 20 minutes or until the lentils are soft and have absorbed most of the water. Season and keep warm in a serving bowl.

4 While that is cooking, prepare the curried vegetables. Take a large pan, heat the oil and fry the chili or chili powder, the ginger, coriander, cumin and salt. Cook this mixture for a few minutes, stirring frequently.

5 When you have done this, put in the vegetables and turn them around in the pan so that they are well coated with the spices. Add a little water and then cook them for 10-20 minutes (depending on which ones you are using) until they are ready. Serve the lentils and vegetables in separate dishes, with rice.

rajma

serves **2-3**

red kidney beans in sauce

1 cup / 225 g red kidney beans, cooked (retain the cooking water)

1 teaspoon cumin seeds

1 onion, sliced thinly

2 cloves garlic, crushed

$1/2$ teaspoon fresh ginger, grated

1 green chili, chopped finely

$1/2$ teaspoon garam masala

1 teaspoon ground coriander

$1/2$ teaspoon turmeric

3-4 tomatoes or 1 can tomatoes

sugar to taste

1 tablespoon fresh cilantro/coriander leaves, chopped

oil

salt

1 Heat the oil and fry the cumin seeds until they begin to jump and turn darker. Add the onion, garlic, ginger and chili. Stirring all the time, cook the mixture for a few minutes.

2 The garam masala, ground coriander and turmeric go in next. Stir well and continue frying for a few minutes. Put in the tomatoes and cook for 5 minutes, stirring from time to time.

3 Drain the beans. Take out about half and mash with a fork in a bowl.

4 Now add all the beans to the tomato mixture and combine well. If it looks too dry, add some of the retained bean water.

5 Bring the pan to the boil and season, adding sugar if using. Cook for 10-20 minutes to let the flavors blend. Serve with the fresh cilantro/coriander leaves scattered on top.

nauratan pullao

serves **2-4**

mixed vegetable pilaff

2 cups / 450 g basmati or other long-grain rice, soaked for 30 minutes in cold water

4-8 tablespoons / 50-100 g margarine or ghee

$^1/_2$ teaspoon cumin seeds

1 medium onion, finely sliced

8 whole black peppercorns

4 cardamom pods

2 bayleaves

half a stick of cinnamon, crushed or $^1/_2$ teaspoon ground cinnamon

4 cloves

2 cups / 300 g mixed vegetables, diced into small pieces of similar size*

$^1/_2$ teaspoon chili powder

salt and pepper

*You can use cauliflower, carrots, peas, okra, tomatoes, beans, turnips or whatever you like – frozen mixed vegetables will do.

1 To begin, heat the margarine or ghee in a large heavy pan. When it has melted add the cumin seeds and cook them for a few seconds before putting in the onions. Stir for 3-5 minutes until the onions are soft.

2 Now add the peppercorns, cardamom pods, bayleaves, cinnamon and cloves and cook for about 3 minutes, stirring from time to time.

3 Put in the vegetables next, and the salt, pepper and chili powder. Stir to mix them and then reduce the heat, cover and simmer gently for 2 minutes.

4 When this is done add the drained rice and stir it into the other ingredients. Pour in enough water to cover the rice mixture by 1 inch/2.5 cm. Cover the pan, bring to the boil and then reduce the heat and simmer undisturbed for 20 minutes or until the water has been absorbed. Serve at once.

samosas

serves **2-4**

FILLING

1 small onion, chopped finely

2 cloves garlic, crushed

1 tablespoon oil

$1/2$ cup / 85 g peas

1 medium potato, parboiled and diced

1 carrot, diced finely

$1/2$ teaspoon garam masala

$1/2$ teaspoon chili powder

small handful fresh cilantro/coriander leaves, chopped

salt and pepper

PASTRY

1 cup / 125 g plain flour

$1/4$ cup / 60 ml water

2 teaspoons oil

OR USE

$1/2$ pound / 225 g frozen plain pastry, thawed

1 First of all, make the pastry by mixing the flour with the water and oil. Leave it to stand for 30 minutes.

2 For the filling, sauté the onion and garlic in the oil and then add the spices and cook for 2 minutes. Now put in the other vegetables and cilantro/coriander and cook them until they are soft. Leave to cool.

3 After that divide the pastry into 2 pieces and roll each portion out on a floured board into a thin rectangular shape, roughly 12 x 6 inches/30 x 15 cms. The pastry should not be too thick.

4 Cut the pastry into strips measuring 2 x 6 inches/5 x 15 cms. Put a small amount of the filling in the center of each strip and fold up into the shape of a triangle. Seal the edges with a little water.

5 Cook the samosas in shallow oil over a medium heat until they are golden brown, or alternatively place them on an oiled broiling/grill pan and dot each with a little margarine. Broil/grill under a medium heat, turning a few times so they do not catch.

kao pad

serves **4-6**

pineapple filled with rice

1 large pineapple

1 pound / 450 g rice, cooked and kept warm

3 tablespoons oil

1 egg, beaten

1 medium onion, sliced finely

1 tablespoon soy sauce

³/₄ cup / 100 g cashew nuts

1 fresh red chili, sliced thinly

1 tablespoon fresh cilantro/coriander or parsley, chopped

salt and pepper

1 Cut a thin lengthwise slice off the pineapple and set aside. Scoop out the flesh while keeping the shell intact to serve the meal in. Cut the fruit into chunks, keeping any juice.

2 Next, heat the oil in a wok or pan and then pour in the beaten egg, circling the wok to distribute evenly. Cook the egg for a few minutes on one side, then turn it over and cook the other side. Remove from the pan and cut it into thin strips.

3 Then stir-fry the onion for 2-3 minutes until it is golden and soft. Add the soy sauce and the rice and cook for 3 minutes. Now put in the pineapple pieces and juice, nuts and strips of egg. Cook for 2 minutes, stirring well. Season with salt and pepper.

4 Fill the scooped-out pineapple with the mixture, add the chili and the cilantro/coriander or parsley. Place on a dish and add any remaining mix around the pineapple.

cadju curry

serves **4**

cashew nut curry

1 cinnamon stick

1 clove

1 cardamom pod

3-4 curry leaves or 1 stalk lemon grass*

1/2 onion, finely sliced

3 cloves garlic, crushed

1 teaspoon fenugreek seeds, crushed

2 teaspoons ground coriander

1 teaspoon ground cumin

1 teaspoon chili powder

1/4 teaspoon turmeric

2 cups / 250 g cashew nuts

1 3/4 cups / 420 ml coconut milk

oil

salt

*Lemon grass can be found in health food stores or Chinese supermarkets.

1 First heat the oil in a heavy pan and fry the cinnamon, clove, cardamom and curry leaves or lemon grass for a few moments before adding the onion and garlic.

2 The ground fenugreek seeds, coriander, cumin, chili, turmeric and cashews go in now; stir well.

3 Let everything cook together for 5 minutes to combine well. Then slowly pour in the coconut milk and stir round. Season, and simmer gently for 10 minutes before serving with boiled rice into which a few raisins or sultanas have been thrown while cooking.

latin
america
& caribbean

empanadas serves **4-6**

pastries

- **¹/₂ pound / 225 g frozen flaky pastry, thawed**
- **1 onion, finely chopped**
- **2 tomatoes, chopped**
- **1 green bell pepper, finely chopped**
- **1 tablespoon chives, chopped**
- **1 pear, finely sliced**
- **2 peaches, finely sliced**
- **¹/₂ cup / 110 g red lentils, cooked**
- **1 tablespoon sugar⁺**
- **¹/₄ cup / 60 ml dry white wine⁺**
- **¹/₂ teaspoon cinnamon**
- **2 tablespoons margarine**
- **salt and pepper**

⁺optional ingredients

Heat oven to 400°F/200°C/Gas 6

1 Heat the margarine and fry the onion until soft. Then put in the tomatoes, bell pepper and chives; stir, and cook for 5 minutes or so.

2 Now add the pear, peaches, and lentils and mix well. Sprinkle in some sugar and pour in wine to taste. Add a little cinnamon and then season.

3 Roll out the pastry and cut to make circles about 4 inches/10 cms in diameter (a saucer is good for this).

4 Put some of the filling on one half of the circle and then moisten the edges with a little water. Fold over the other half and press the two sides together with the back of a fork. Make a couple of punctures in the top to let the steam escape.

5 Fill the other empanadas and then place them on a baking tray in the oven for about 20 minutes until the pastry is puffed up and golden. Serve at once with a green salad.

BOLIVIA

locro

serves **6**

squash/pumpkin stew

2 pounds / 1 kg squash, pumpkin or sweet potato, peeled and cut into 1 inch/2.5 cm chunks

1/2 cup / 120 ml water

1 onion, chopped

1 tomato, chopped

1/2 teaspoon oregano

1-2 cobs of corn, cut into 2 inch/5 cm pieces

1 pound / 450 g potatoes, cut into cubes and parboiled

1/2 cup / 85 g habas, butter beans or Lima beans, cooked

1/2 cup / 85 g peas

1 cup / 100 g feta or other crumbly cheese

1 tablespoon fresh parsley, chopped

oil

salt and pepper

1 Put the water into a pan with the squash, pumpkin or sweet potato and bring it to the boil; cook until it begins to soften.

2 While that is happening, heat the oil in another pan and sauté the onion and then add the tomato, oregano and salt and pepper. Put this mixture into the squash and combine well.

3 The corn, potatoes and beans go in now. Let them cook gently in the squash stew for 10 minutes or so and then add the peas.

4 When the corn is cooked, crumble in the cheese or cut it into cubes and add these. Heat through and stir carefully until the cheese begins to melt. Now cast the chopped parsley on top and serve right away.

serves **4-6**

frijoles refritos

fried beans

2 cups / 450 g
**black or red kidney
beans, cooked**

**¹/₄ teaspoon
chili powder**

1 onion, chopped finely

**1 cup / 100 g grated
cheese**

3 tomatoes, chopped

**¹/₂ teaspoon fresh basil
or parsley, chopped**

oil

salt and pepper

1 Place the beans in a bowl and mash them with a fork, or use a blender. Sprinkle on the chili powder, season and mix well again.

2 Then heat the oil and cook the onion so that it softens. Add the bean mash and fry it over a gentle heat, stirring all the time, until it has a firm consistency.

3 Transfer the beans to a serving dish, scatter the grated cheese over and keep hot.

4 Now make a sauce by placing the chopped tomatoes, basil or parsley, seasoning, and a little water if necessary and chili powder if liked, into a saucepan or blender and mix well. Heat it up and serve alongside the frijoles together with rice or corn chips/nachos.

CARIBBEAN

rice & peas

1 cup / 225 g pigeon peas*, soaked

1 onion, sliced finely

1 pound / 450 g rice

1/2 cup / 120 ml coconut milk

1/4 teaspoon thyme

1/4 teaspoon oregano

1/2 teaspoon chili powder

salt

*A quicker version is to use canned red kidney beans. Simply add them to the rice which has been cooked with the other ingredients.

1 To begin with, put the peas in a pan with the onion and enough water to cover. Bring this to the boil and then add 2 cups/470 ml water. Cover with a lid, bring to the boil again; this time allow it to simmer until the pigeon peas are tender, about 1 hour.

2 After this, add the coconut milk, herbs, chili powder and salt, stirring well to mix them.

3 Put in the rice, adding more water if necessary and bring to the boil. Then reduce the heat and cook the rice until it is done, about 20-30 minutes. Season and serve.

CARIBBEAN

serves **4-6**

pumpkin curry

1 pound / 450 g pumpkin,
cut into small cubes

¹/₂ tablespoon turmeric

1 green chili,
chopped finely

1 onion, chopped

5 cloves garlic, chopped

1 teaspoon ground ginger
or ¹/₂ teaspoon fresh
ginger, grated

2-3 cloves

2 tomatoes, chopped

1¹/₄ cups / 300 ml
coconut milk

oil

salt

1 First, boil the pumpkin pieces in a little water for 15 minutes or until they are tender. Drain.

2 Now heat the oil and put in the turmeric and chili. Stir round for 30 seconds before adding the onion. Cook until the onion is soft and then put in the garlic, ginger, cloves and tomatoes. Simmer this for 5 minutes over a low heat, stirring from time to time.

3 The pumpkin goes in now. Mix it in well with the spices and continue to cook at a low heat for 15 minutes.

4 Pour in the coconut milk and stir to blend it in, adding salt to taste. Heat through gently.

CHILE

porotos

serves **4**

bean and pumpkin stew

1 onion, sliced

2 cloves garlic, crushed

$1/2$ teaspoon chili powder

$1/2$ teaspoon cumin seeds

4-6 tomatoes, chopped

1 cup / 225 g white kidney or flageolet beans, cooked

1 pound / 450 g pumpkin*, cubed and cooked (retain the cooking water)

$1/2$ pound / 225 g spaghetti

1 tablespoon fresh basil, chopped

oil

salt and pepper

*Or use sweet potato.

1 First, heat the oil and gently fry the onion until it is soft and transparent. Then put in the garlic, chili powder and cumin seeds and cook for a couple of minutes before adding the chopped tomatoes.

2 When the tomatoes have softened, the beans and pumpkin can be added, together with some of the pumpkin water if you wish.

3 Season, cover, and leave to stew for a few minutes while you cook the spaghetti in boiling water according to the packet instructions.

4 Once the pasta is ready, drain it and then transfer to a serving dish or spoon it onto plates and ladle the stew over. Garnish with the fresh basil.

ochos rios

serves **4**

coconut rice and beans

1 onion, sliced

¹/₂ cup / 120 ml stock

¹/₂ chili, finely chopped

¹/₂ teaspoon thyme

**¹/₂ cup / 110 g
rice, cooked**

**¹/₂ cup / 110 g kidney
beans, cooked**

**1 cup / 75 g dried/
desiccated coconut**

2-3 tablespoons milk

oil

salt

1 To begin, sauté the onion in the heated oil and then put in the stock, chili, thyme and a little salt. Cover and bring to the boil.

2 Now add the cooked beans and rice, followed by the coconut. Stir well and then let the mixture simmer, uncovered, for about 20 minutes so that the ingredients and flavors blend well.

3 After this, stir in the milk and heat the mixture through gently before serving accompanied by a green salad and/or chutney.

menestra de lentejas

serves **4-6**

lentil stew

$^1/_2$ pound / 225 g green lentils, cooked

2 onions, chopped finely

1$^1/_2$ teaspoons ground cumin

1 green bell pepper, chopped

1 tablespoon fresh parsley, chopped

1 tablespoon fresh cilantro/coriander leaves, chopped

1 can tomatoes

oil

salt and pepper

1 Heat the oil and sauté the onions for a minute or two before adding the cumin, bell pepper, parsley and cilantro/coriander.

2 When they are all soft and integrated, add the cooked lentils and the tinned tomatoes with their liquid. Stir the mixture well.

3 Bring the pot to the boil and simmer very gently, stirring from time to time so that the lentils do not catch, until the stew is thick. Add water as required to make the consistency you prefer.

llapingachos serves **6**

potato cakes with peanut sauce

2 onions, finely chopped

2 pounds / 1 kg potatoes, mashed

2 tablespoons fresh parsley, chopped

2 cups / 200 g cheddar or monterrey jack cheese, grated

¹/₂ cup / 110 g peanut butter

¹/₂ cup / 120 ml stock or water

6 eggs

lemon juice

a few lettuce leaves

2 tablespoons margarine

oil

salt and pepper

1 Melt the margarine and cook the onions until they are soft.

2 Transfer them to a bowl when ready and combine them with the mashed potatoes, parsley and cheese, adding salt and pepper to taste.

3 Now shape this potato mixture into cakes about 1 inch/2.5 cm thick. Heat a little oil in a frying pan or use a griddle. When it is very hot, cook the cakes until they are golden on one side and then turn them over to brown the other side. Keep the potato cakes warm.

4 Spoon the peanut butter into a small saucepan and add the stock, stirring well so that it is evenly absorbed. Heat gently.

5 Now poach the eggs in a little water. To serve, place the potato cakes on a dish lined with lettuce leaves, slide the eggs on top and pass the peanut sauce round separately.

serves **4**

filled egg-plant

2 egg-plants/aubergines, halved lengthwise

1 onion, chopped

2 slices bread, diced, and soaked in 1 cup / 240 ml milk

1 egg

2 cups / 200 g monterrey jack or cheddar cheese, grated

2 heaped tablespoons breadcrumbs or sesame seeds

oil

salt and pepper

Heat oven to 350°F/180°C/Gas 4

1 Boil the egg-plant/aubergine halves in a little water for 5 minutes or so. Drain. When cool, remove the pulp and cut into small chunks. Keep the egg-plant/aubergine shells.

2 Heat the oil in a pan and cook the onion until it is soft; then add the egg-plant/aubergine pieces and cook for about 5 minutes.

3 Squeeze the bread and put it into the onion mixture, adding salt and pepper. Mix ingredients well. Remove the pan from the heat.

4 Beat egg in a small bowl and then pour into the pan containing the onion and egg-plant/aubergine mix. Add half the cheese and mix well.

5 Place the egg-plant/aubergine shells on a greased oven-proof dish; pile the mixture into them. Top with remaining cheese and scatter the breadcrumbs or sesame seeds over. Bake for 15-20 minutes.

serves **2-4**

avocado tacos

FOR THE FILLING:

2 avocados

2 cloves garlic, crushed

$1/2$ teaspoon chili powder

2 teaspoons lime or lemon juice

1 tomato, chopped

1 onion, cut in circles

1 cup / 100 g monterrey jack or cheddar cheese, grated

FOR THE TACOS:

1 cup / 125 g masa harina* and water to make a soft dough

OR USE

6 taco shells

*Available in some specialist foodstores.

1 To make the filling, scoop out the avocado pulp into a bowl and combine with the garlic, chili powder and lime or lemon juice.

2 Now prepare the tacos by mixing the masa harina with enough water to make a malleable dough. Then divide and roll it into golf-ball size pieces. If the dough seems too moist, cover the balls with a tea towel and let them sit for 10-20 minutes.

3 After this, roll the balls out flat. Then heat a griddle without oil and cook the tacos until they are lightly browned on both sides.

4 Quickly fill each one by placing a spoon of filling, topped with a little onion, tomato and cheese, on one half of the taco. Then fold over.

5 When filled, you can eat them straight away or fry them on both sides in a little oil until crisp. Drain on kitchen paper before serving with hot sauce, rice and salad.

enchiladas de frijoles

serves **4**

bean tortillas

1 cup / 150 g red or black beans, cooked and kept warm

1 onion, chopped

1 clove garlic, chopped

1 dried chili, chopped finely

4 tomatoes, chopped

1/2 green bell pepper, chopped

1/4 pound / 110 g monterrey jack or cheddar cheese, grated+

6 tortillas or 8 taco shells

1-2 tablespoons fresh cilantro/coriander leaves or parsley, chopped

1 tablespoon margarine

salt and pepper

+optional ingredient

Heat oven to
250°F/130°C/Gas 1/2

1 First heat the margarine and sauté the onion, adding the garlic, chili, tomatoes and green bell pepper once the onion is transparent. Cook for 5 minutes.

2 While that is cooking, mash the beans with a little salt and pepper.

3 When almost ready to serve, divide the mixture among the tortillas, placing it along the center. Then roll up the tortilla and secure with an orange stick or small kebab skewer. If using taco shells, simply fill them.

4 Place on a shallow dish and pour the sauce over. Serve at once with salad. Top with grated cheese, and the cilantro/coriander or parsley.

avocado & bean salad

serves **4**

1 cup / 100 g red kidney beans, soaked, cooked and cooled

1 large avocado

1 clove garlic, crushed

1/4 teaspoon chili powder

1 tablespoon olive oil

1 tablespoon lemon juice or vinegar

a few lettuce leaves, washed and dried

1 small onion, sliced finely into circles

1 small red or green bell pepper, sliced in rounds

4 hard-boiled eggs, sliced

1/4 teaspoon paprika

salt and pepper

1 First make a lengthwise slit round the avocado to open it. Then, using a spoon, scoop the flesh into a bowl and mash. Add the garlic, chili powder, oil, lemon juice or vinegar, salt and pepper and mix to a creamy consistency.

2 Now partially mash the beans with a fork.

3 Place the lettuce leaves on a large plate, spoon on the beans and then the avocado mixture. Top with the onion circles, pepper and egg slices and sprinkle on the paprika before serving.

molletes

serves **4**

chili bean snack

1 stick of French bread

1 cup / 225 g black or red kidney beans, cooked

1/2 pound / 225 g cheddar or monterrey jack cheese, grated

1/4 chili, chopped finely or 1/2 teaspoon chili powder

water

oil

salt and pepper

Heat oven to 350°F/180°C/Gas 4

1 First slice the French bread into 4 sections and then slice each piece in half lengthwise. Scoop out some of the bread from each piece to make 8 'boats' or cradles which will later be filled with beans.

2 Put the beans in a bowl, add the chili powder, the salt and pepper and also a little water. Partially mash the beans with a fork.

3 Next, heat up the oil in a large pan and when it is very hot, fry the mashed beans to make frijoles refritos (refried beans). You may need to do this in more than one batch unless the pan is very large.

4 When the beans are ready, fill the hollows in the bread with the mixture and top with the grated cheese.

5 Place the bread sections on a baking tray and cook in the oven until they have heated through and the cheese is golden on top. Serve with salad.

papas à la huancaina

serves **4-6**

huancaina-style potatoes

10 medium potatoes, cooked and sliced

1 small onion, finely chopped

4 hard-boiled eggs

1/2 cup / 100 g ricotta or cottage cheese, sieved

2 teaspoons chili powder

2 tablespoons single cream or evaporated milk

3 tablespoons oil

juice of half a lemon

10 black or green olives

handful fresh parsley, chopped

salt and pepper

1 Boil a little water in a pan and cook the onion in it for a few minutes, and then drain.

2 Take out the yolks from 2 of the eggs and mash them in a bowl, using a fork. Then add the ricotta or cottage cheese and season with the chili powder, salt and pepper. When this is done, stir in the cream or evaporated milk and mix well before adding the oil, lemon juice and cooked onion.

3 Arrange the potato slices on a flat dish. Cover them with the cheese sauce and then garnish with the olives, slices of hard-boiled egg and parsley.

middle
east &
north
africa

thetchouka

serves **4**

baked omelet

1 onion, chopped

3 cloves garlic, crushed

1 chili, sliced

2 bell peppers, sliced into thin strips lengthwise

6 tomatoes, chopped

4 eggs, beaten

oil

salt and pepper

1 If you have one, use a pan that can transfer to the oven. Heat the oil and cook the onion for a few minutes before adding the garlic, chili and bell peppers.

2 When they have softened, put in the tomatoes and the seasoning. Let the mixture cook for 5 minutes, and stir from time to time.

3 Now pour the beaten eggs on top and bake in the oven for 10-15 minutes or until the eggs are set as you like them.

Heat oven to 350°F/180°C/Gas 4

ALGERIA

vegetable couscous

serves **4-6**

1 pound / 450 g couscous

2 onions, chopped

1/2 pound / 225 g carrots, sliced

1/2 pound / 225 g pumpkin, squash or turnip, cut into chunks

1/2 teaspoon ginger

1 cup / 175 g peas and/or cooked chickpeas

3 zucchini/courgettes, sliced

1 egg-plant/aubergine, sliced

1 cup / 100 g raisins or sultanas

3 tomatoes, chopped

1/2 teaspoon chili powder

2 teaspoons paprika

2 tablespoons fresh cilantro/coriander leaves or parsley, chopped

1-2 teaspoons harissa*

oil

salt and pepper

*Or substitute 1 tablespoon paprika mixed with 1 teaspoon of chili powder and 2 teaspoons of ground allspice.

1 Use a saucepan which will be deep enough for a sieve containing the couscous to sit across the top without it touching the vegetables, or use a couscousière.

2 Put the onions, carrots and pumpkin into the pan first, as these take longer to cook. Cover with water and a little oil, ginger and pepper and simmer for 20 minutes.

3 Then add the peas or chickpeas, zucchini/courgettes, egg-plant/aubergine, raisins or sultanas, tomatoes, chili powder, paprika, cilantro/coriander or parsley and stir well.

4 Now, if using a saucepan, put the couscous into the sieve and rest this across the top of the pan. Put the saucepan lid above it and steam for 30 minutes or as necessary, as the vegetables cook underneath.

(Many varieties of couscous are pre-cooked so follow the packet instructions.) If you choose to cook the couscous in a separate pan, just part-cook it and then transfer to the sieve for 10 minutes to imbibe the vegetable flavor from the steam.

5 For the sauce, remove 6 tablespoons of the broth and put in a bowl. Stir in 1-2 teaspoons of harissa (or the substitute paste mixture) and mix well. Serve the sauce separately.

6 When ready, pile the couscous grains in a bowl and make a well in the center. Fill with the vegetable mix and sprinkle on the cilantro/coriander leaves. Serve with yogurt and tomato salad.

falafel

makes **20**

spicy cakes

2¹/₂ cups / 450 g chickpeas or white broad beans, soaked and cooked

2 cloves garlic, crushed

1 medium onion, grated

handful fresh cilantro/ coriander leaves or parsley, chopped

1 teaspoon ground cumin

1 teaspoon ground coriander

¹/₂ teaspoon cayenne pepper

¹/₂ teaspoon turmeric

¹/₂ teaspoon baking powder

lemon juice

sesame seeds

a little flour

oil for cooking

water

salt and pepper

1 Mince, pound or put the beans/ chickpeas through a blender until they are very smooth. This is important since the falafel will not bind well otherwise.

2 Now put in all the other ingredients except the sesame seeds, flour and oil. Leave to stand for at least 15 minutes; 1 hour if possible.

3 Now take small amounts of the mixture and make round cakes about 2 inches/5 cms in diameter and ³/₄ inch/1.5 cm thick. Add a little flour and water if they are not binding well.

4 Leave them to rest for 15 minutes and then press a few sesame seeds on top of each one.

5 Next, heat the oil in a pan and brown the falafel for a few minutes on each side, until golden brown. Drain on absorbent paper and serve hot with pitta bread, yogurt and slices of tomato or salad.

ful medames serves 4

brown beans with eggs

1 cup / 225 g ful brown beans, soaked

1 quart / 1 liter water

4 cloves garlic, crushed

1 tablespoon ground cumin

6 hard-boiled eggs, halved

1 teaspoon turmeric

2 tablespoons fresh parsley, chopped

4 tomatoes, sliced

2 lemons, cut into wedges

1 teaspoon paprika

6 tablespoons olive oil

salt

Heat oven to 300°F/150°C/Gas 2

1 Place the beans in an ovenproof casserole on top of the cooker with the water, garlic, 3 tablespoons of the oil and the cumin. Heat up and when the water is boiling, cover the pan and boil for 10 minutes.

2 Transfer the beans to the oven and let them cook very slowly for 3-4 hours (less if they are partially cooked already) until they are soft. Season.

3 Put the hard-boiled eggs on a plate and dust them with the turmeric. Pour the olive oil into a jug or dish (or use the bottle); arrange the tomato slices, parsley and lemon wedges on dishes to be handed round separately.

4 Sprinkle the paprika on the ful before bringing the casserole to the table. Place the side dish ingredients around it so people can help themselves.

labaneya

serves **6**

yogurt and spinach soup

1 onion, sliced

2 pounds / 1 kg spinach,
torn into strips

¹/₂ cup / 110 g rice

2 cups / 440 g yogurt

2-3 cloves garlic,
crushed

3 tablespoons oil

1 quart / 1 liter
warm water

salt and pepper

1 Using a large pan, heat the oil and then add the onion and cook until it is soft.

2 Now put in the spinach and combine it with the onion; cook them gently for about 10 minutes.

3 The rice goes in now. Stir it in to the onion and spinach mixture and then pour in the water, salt and pepper. Bring to the boil and let the rice simmer for 10-20 minutes until it is soft. Take the pan off the heat.

4 Turn the yogurt into a bowl and beat it with the crushed garlic. When that is done, spoon the yogurt mix into the soup and stir well. Then return the saucepan to the heat and cook very gently just to warm the soup. Take care not to let it boil as this will curdle the yogurt.

serves **4**

red bean & spinach stew

¹/₄ pound / 110 g red kidney beans, cooked (keep the cooking liquid)

¹/₄ pound / 110 g red lentils

1 pound / 450 g spinach, chopped

¹/₄ cup / 60 g rice

2 onions, chopped finely

1 teaspoon turmeric

¹/₂ teaspoon chili powder

¹/₂ teaspoon ground cumin

1 teaspoon ground coriander

4 cups / 1 liter water

juice of 2 lemons

oil

salt and pepper

1 Heat the oil and sauté the onions until they are translucent.

2 Now mix in the turmeric, chili powder, cumin and coriander before adding the lentils and rice. Stir these round for a minute to coat them lightly in the oil.

3 Next put in the water and seasoning. Cover the pan and bring to the boil.

4 When boiling, reduce the heat and simmer gently for 15 minutes until the lentils are almost ready.

5 At this point, add the cooked beans and their liquid as well as the spinach. Return to the boil, reduce the heat, cover and simmer for 15 minutes to let the flavors amalgamate. Stir in the lemon juice and serve with yogurt.

IRAN

kukuye sabzi serves **4**
vegetable and walnut bake

2 cups / 200 g leeks,
chopped finely

1 cup / 150 g lettuce,
chopped finely

1 tablespoon fresh
parsley, chopped

1 cup / 100 g spinach,
chopped finely

3 scallions / spring
onions, sliced finely

1 tablespoon flour

1/2 cup / 60 g walnuts,
chopped

8 eggs

4 tablespoons / 50 g
margarine

salt and pepper

Heat oven to
325°F/160°C/Gas 3

1 Put all the vegetables into a large bowl, shake on the flour and seasoning. Mix well and then add the walnuts.

2 Next, beat the eggs and pour them into the vegetable mixture. Stir so that the egg coats the other ingredients to bind them.

3 Using a loaf tin, melt the margarine gently over a low heat and swirl it around the pan to coat the sides. Then transfer the vegetable mixture to the tin and cook in the oven for about 1 hour or until the top is crisp and brown. Turn out onto a dish and serve with rice and yogurt.

JORDAN

basal badawi <small>serves 4</small>

onions with lentils, nuts and fruit

4 large onions

¹/₂ cup / 100 g red lentils, cooked

³/₄ cup / 150 ml plain yogurt

2 tablespoons dates, stoned and finely chopped

2 tablespoons walnuts, chopped

1 tablespoon raisins or sultanas

2 tablespoons breadcrumbs

handful fresh parsley, chopped

salt and pepper

Heat oven to 375°F/190°C/Gas 5

1 Peel the onions and place them in a large pan of boiling water. Reduce the heat and let them simmer for 15-20 minutes, covered, until they are fairly tender. When they are ready, take them out and set aside to cool.

2 Now remove the center section of each onion to leave a shell about ³/₄ inch/1.5 cm thick.

3 In a bowl mix together the lentils, pepper, salt, yogurt, dates, walnuts, raisins or sultanas and breadcrumbs.

4 Fill the onions with this mixture. Keep any that remains and mix it with the chopped discarded onion centers.

5 Place the filled onions in an oven-proof dish, spoon any remaining mixture around them and cook for about 20 minutes. Garnish with parsley and serve with bulghur or rice.

maraga bil-tomatich

serves **4**

tomato and lentil sauce

1 cup / 225 g red lentils

6 large tomatoes, chopped

1 teaspoon tomato paste

3 tablespoons water

2-4 cloves garlic, sliced finely or crushed

handful fresh parsley, chopped

1 large onion, grated

2 tablespoons margarine

1 teaspoon sugar

1/2 teaspoon thyme

1 bayleaf, crushed

lemon juice

salt and pepper

1 First, mix the tomato paste with the water. Then pour it into a large pan containing the lentils and rest of the ingredients.

2 Cover the saucepan and cook very gently for 20 minutes, stirring regularly to prevent sticking.

3 After this, remove the pan from the heat and leave it to cool. Mash the ingredients with a wooden spoon adding lemon juice and a little water to make a moist mixture.

4 Return the mixture to the pan and boil for a few minutes. Serve with pasta or rice and salad.

MIDDLE EAST

reuchta mubowakh

serves **4**

noodles with chickpeas

1 pound / 450 g noodles

1 tablespoon / 25 g margarine

1 large onion, chopped

2 large tomatoes, chopped

2 tablespoons tomato paste

1 cup / 175 g chickpeas, soaked and cooked

$1/4$ teaspoon saffron, soaked in 4 tablespoons water[+]

$1/2$ teaspoon paprika

4 cups / 950 ml water

salt and pepper

[+]optional ingredient or use $1/2$ teaspoon turmeric

1 Melt the margarine in a pan and cook the onion until it is soft. Add the chopped tomatoes, and the tomato paste diluted in 5 tablespoons of the water. Cook for 5 minutes.

2 Next put in the chickpeas, spices and remaining water and bring to the boil, stirring frequently. After this, reduce the heat, season and let the sauce bubble very slowly while you cook the pasta.

3 Break the pasta into small pieces, about 2 inches/5 cms long, and place them in a fine-meshed metal sieve. Rest the sieve on the rim of the pan and sit the lid on top. The pasta should cook in the steam of the sauce. Lower the heat now and simmer for about 20 minutes. Every few minutes take out a ladleful of liquid and sauce pour it over the pasta – it is this which gives the unusual texture and flavor.

4 When the pasta is ready, put into a serving bowl, pour the sauce over and serve with a green salad.

mahasha

serves **4**

stuffed tomatoes

4 marmande or other large tomatoes

2 tablespoons fresh cilantro/coriander leaves, chopped

1/2 pound / 225 g potatoes, mashed

1/3 cup / 60 g peas

1 teaspoon curry powder

1/2-1 teaspoon chili powder

2 teaspoons cumin seeds

1 teaspoon mustard seeds

1 clove garlic, crushed

oil

salt

Heat oven to 325°F/160°C/Gas 3

1 To begin, slice the tomatoes in half and carefully scoop out the pulp and seeds; keep these for later use.

2 Then heat up some oil in a pan and when it is very hot, toss in the cilantro/coriander leaves and let them crisp up.

3 Now add the curry powder, chili, cumin seeds, mustard seeds and garlic to the fried cilantro/coriander leaves. Mix well and sprinkle on salt as required.

4 Cook for a minute or two before adding the mashed potato or bulghur, the peas and the tomato pulp. Stir all the ingredients well to distribute the spices.

5 Fill the tomatoes with the mixture and place them in a shallow ovenproof dish. Bake for 15-20 minutes and serve hot or cold.

MOROCCO

COUSCOUS

serves **4-6**

$^1/_2$ cup / 85 g chickpeas, cooked (keep the water)

$^1/_2$ cup / 60 g white cabbage, finely sliced

1 onion, chopped

1 cup / 150 g turnip, chopped+

1 carrot, sliced

3 cloves

1 teaspoon cinnamon

$^1/_2$ teaspoon ground ginger

1 teaspoon paprika

2 zucchini/courgettes, sliced

1 egg-plant/aubergine, chopped

4 tomatoes, cut into quarters

$^1/_2$ cup / 50 g sultanas or raisins

2 tablespoons fresh cilantro/coriander leaves, chopped

$^1/_4$ teaspoon chili powder

$^1/_4$ cup / 50 ml tomato juice

$^1/_2$ pound / 225 g couscous

1 tablespoon margarine or oil

salt and pepper

+optional ingredient

1 To begin, shake the couscous into a bowl and dampen it with a little warm water. Stir it and leave the grain to swell for about 15 minutes.

2 Now put the chickpeas and their water in a large pan and add the cabbage, onion, turnip and carrot together with the cloves, cinnamon, ginger and paprika. Bring to the boil and cook until the vegetables are almost tender.

3 The zucchini/courgettes, egg-plant/aubergine, tomatoes, sultanas or raisins, cilantro/coriander leaves, chili powder and tomato juice can all go in at this point, along with the salt and pepper.

4 Place the couscous into a sieve (with a lid over) or couscousière and steam it above the cooking vegetables for 20-30 minutes.

5 When everything is ready, spoon the couscous into a warmed serving dish and mix in a little margarine. Serve the vegetables separately.

khboz

serves **4**

spicy spinach and cheese pastries

1 pound / 450g frozen plain pastry, thawed

3 tablespoons / 40 g margarine, melted

$1/2$ teaspoon cumin

1 tablespoon paprika

$1/2$ teaspoon chili powder

2 cloves garlic, crushed

2 cups / 200 g spinach or parsley, chopped finely

2 onions, chopped finely

2 cups / 225 g feta or other crumbly cheese

salt and pepper

Heat oven to 375°F/190°C/Gas 5

1 Combine the melted margarine, cumin, paprika, chili powder, garlic, spinach or parsley and onions. Add seasoning.

2 Divide the pastry into 8 pieces and knead each one. Then, on a floured surface, roll each piece into a rectangle 8 x 6 inches/20 x 15 cms.

3 Divide the filling equally between the portions. Crumble some of the cheese on each.

4 Fold the two short sides of the pastry rectangle into the middle so they just meet over the filling. Then roll the cake up, beginning with one of the long sides. Seal each end with water and press together with a fork.

5 Put the khboz on a baking sheet and bake for 35 minutes or until slightly browned. Serve hot with salad.

bean stew

serves **4-6**

tajine with black-eyed beans

1/2 pound / 225 g black-eyed beans, cooked (save the liquid)

1 onion, chopped

1 red bell pepper, chopped

1 green bell pepper, chopped

4 tomatoes, chopped

2 tablespoons tomato paste

1 teaspoon cinnamon

1/2 teaspoon grated nutmeg

1 pound / 450 g spinach, chopped

oil

salt and pepper

1 Fry the onion in the oil until it is transparent. Then add the red and green bell peppers and cook until they soften.

2 Now put in the tomatoes, tomato paste, cinnamon and nutmeg and stir well.

3 Add the beans and stir them into the mixture. Then season with pepper and salt before placing the spinach on top. Add a little water or retained cooking liquid and stew for 20 minutes.

lentil &
spinach stew

serves **6**

¹/₂ pound / 225 g
red lentils

1 pound / 450 g spinach,
chopped finely

1 onion, sliced finely

4 cloves garlic, crushed

1 teaspoon ground cumin

juice of 1 lemon

water

oil

salt and pepper

1 Taking a large pan, heat the oil and cook the onion until it is soft and golden; then add the garlic and cumin.

2 Now put in the lentils, cover with water and bring to the boil. Remove any scum on the surface with a spoon. After about 15 minutes when the lentils are cooked and the water almost gone, add the spinach and stir it in. Season and continue to stir to produce a purée.

3 Cook for 3-5 minutes until the spinach softens. Then add the lemon juice and more water as desired to make the consistency you prefer. Serve with pitta bread and yogurt.

imam bayaldi

serves **4**

stuffed egg-plant/aubergine

4 egg-plants/aubergines

1 onion, finely sliced

4 cloves garlic, crushed

1 green bell pepper, chopped

6 tomatoes, chopped

squeeze of lemon juice

1 tablespoon fresh parsley, chopped

1 cup / 100 g monterrey jack or cheddar cheese, grated

1 cup / 225 g yogurt

oil

salt and pepper

Heat oven to
325°F/160°C/Gas 3

1 First of all, put the egg-plants/aubergines into the oven to cook for 10 minutes or so.

2 While they are baking, heat the oil in a pan and cook the onion until it turns soft and transparent. Now add the garlic and stir this round for a few moments but do not let it brown.

3 The green bell pepper goes in next, and when it has softened put in the tomatoes. Continue to cook gently for a few minutes.

4 Meanwhile, remove the egg-plants/aubergines from the oven and when they are cool enough to handle, cut off the stalk end and slice them in halves, lengthwise.

5 Remove as much of the pulp as you can, using a teaspoon or sharp knife, without damaging the skins. Chop up the pulp and add it to the pan with the onion and other vegetables. Squeeze in some lemon juice and season.

6 Arrange the egg-plant/aubergine halves in an ovenproof dish and pile the cooked mixture into them, and around them if there is some left over.

7 Put the dish into the oven for 10 minutes, with the cheese on top, and cook for a few minutes or until the cheese has melted and turned golden.

8 Remove from the oven, scatter the parsley over and serve either hot or cold, with yogurt.

serves **4-6**

casserole
with egg-plant/aubergine

3 tablespoons olive oil

2 eggs

1 tablespoon milk

1 cup / 110 g kefalotiri, parmesan or cheddar cheese, finely grated

2 medium egg-plants/ aubergines, cut crosswise into thin slices

6 large tomatoes, sliced

2 handfuls fresh parsley, chopped finely

pepper and salt

SAUCE

1 egg

1 small onion, grated

1/2 teaspoon marjoram

2 tablespoons tomato paste

3 tablespoons water

pepper and salt

Heat oven to 350°F/180°C/Gas 4

1 Pour oil into a large shallow pan and heat gently. In a bowl, beat the eggs with the milk, salt and pepper.

2 Dip each egg-plant/aubergine slice into the egg mixture and then cook in the hot oil, turning so they are soft and golden. Drain on paper towels.

3 Place half the slices over the base of a greased shallow oven-proof dish. Arrange a layer of tomato slices on top, and then sprinkle some grated cheese and a little parsley over them.

4 Repeat until egg-plant/aubergine, tomato, cheese and parsley have been used up.

5 Mix or blend the ingredients for the sauce in a bowl adding enough water to make a smooth sauce.

6 Pour evenly over the egg-plant/ aubergine mixture, place the dish in the oven and cook, covered, for 30 minutes. Remove the lid and continue to cook for another 15 minutes so that the top is golden.

herb omelet serves **4-6**

2 handfuls fresh parsley,
chopped

2 handfuls fresh mint,
chopped

1 medium potato, cooked
and diced

1 medium onion,
chopped finely

6 eggs, beaten

1 tablespoon
self-raising flour

2 cloves garlic, crushed

1-2 tablespoons oil

salt and pepper

1 Take a large bowl and mix all the ingredients together, except the oil. The mixture should be thick.

2 Then heat the oil in a large flat pan. When it is hot, spoon in the omelet, moving the pan around so that the mixture is evenly distributed.

3 Cook for a few minutes on one side and then the other. Serve hot or cold.

eggeh

serves **4**

broad bean omelet

2 cups / 225 g broad beans (canned or frozen will do)

6 eggs

4 scallions/spring onions, finely sliced

juice of 1/2 lemon

1 tablespoon margarine or oil

salt and pepper

1 Begin by boiling the beans for a few minutes until they are tender; drain.

2 Then beat the eggs and mix them with the beans, scallions/spring onions, lemon juice, salt and pepper.

3 Heat the oil or margarine in a pan and when it is sizzling pour in the egg and bean mixture. Put a cover on the pan and cook for 15-20 minutes over a gentle heat.

4 To brown the top, place the pan under the grill for a few minutes. The omelet can be served hot or cold, cut into wedges.

TURKEY

pilaff
with apricots and almonds

serves **6-8**

Ingredients

- 3-4 tablespoons oil
- 2 medium onions, finely chopped
- 3 cloves garlic, crushed
- 1 pound / 450 g brown rice
- 3 bayleaves
- 1 can tomatoes, chopped
- 2 tablespoons tomato paste
- 1 cup / 100 g dried apricots
- 1/2 cup / 50 g raisins or sultanas
- 1/2 cup / 60 g flaked almonds
- 2 1/2 cups / 590 ml stock
- 1 tablespoon fresh cilantro/coriander leaves, chopped
- salt and pepper

Method

1 To start, first heat the oil and then soften the onions and garlic in it.

2 Add the rice and fry it for 3 minutes, stirring frequently so that each grain is lightly coated with oil.

3 When this is done, put in the bayleaves, tomatoes and tomato paste, dried fruit, nuts, stock and seasoning.

4 Bring the pan to the boil and then reduce the heat and simmer, covered, for 45 minutes until the rice is cooked and most of the moisture has been absorbed. Serve garnished with chopped coriander leaves.

nutrition facts

With increasing concern about obesity in the West, and poor nutrition in many Majority World countries, it is useful to know what we require from our food – and what we do not need. Buying fair trade and organic produce improves the quality of what we eat while also supporting ethical farming and trading practices.

Humans need carbohydrates, fiber, protein, fat, vitamins and minerals as well as water. These maintain our bodies and give us energy, measured in calories. A person's calorie requirement varies according to their age, health, size and activity level. A small person with a sedentary life may only require 2,000 calories a day, while someone who is large and does heavy physical work may need 3,500. The UN agencies recommend a minimum daily intake (RDI) for adults of 2,300-2,600 calories per person.

Ideally, calories should be drawn from the range of nutrients listed above. The main or macro-nutrients – carbohydrates, protein and fat – provide different amounts of calories. Fat is very high in calories: one gram of oil, butter or margarine supplies nine calories. Carbohydrates (from sugars and starches) and protein (from beans, nuts and dairy foods) provide four calories for each gram. Alcohol delivers seven calories per gram (or milliliter), so a glass of dry white wine would be about 100 calories.

Protein

Protein is the body's building material. It is made up of amino acids; foods contain these in differing proportions. The highest-quality protein foods contain the most complete set of essential amino acids in the right proportions for the body to be able to make the best use of them. According to the American Dietetics Association, 'plant sources of protein alone can provide adequate amounts of essential amino acids if a variety of plant foods are consumed and energy needs are met.' The UN Food and Agriculture Organization recommends that around 10 per cent of a person's energy intake should come from protein. So on the 2,600 RDI calories about 260 should be from protein. Since each gram of protein provides four calories, you would therefore need 65 grams of protein each day, depending on your age, sex, lifestyle and so on. The UN figure leaves a comfortable margin: the Vegetarian Society in Britain suggests that 45 grams per day is plenty for women (more if pregnant, breastfeeding or very active) and 55 grams for men (more if very active).

People in the rich world rarely lack protein because overall we consume well above the 2,600 calories level and within that food intake there is likely to be sufficient protein. It is a different situation in countries where the overall calorie consumption is low (the 500 million people of the least developed countries rarely consume more than 2,000 calories; one of the lowest national averages is Sierra Leone's 1,880).

Vegetarian foods rich in protein include nuts, seeds, pulses (peas, beans, lentils), grains, dairy produce, eggs and soy products such as tofu. Vegetables, salads and fruit contribute small amounts of amino acids as well.

Carbohydrates
Carbohydrates are the main source of energy. In plant foods, these normally come as sugars and starches. Avoid sugars and refined starches (white bread, white rice) as although they bring

calories, they bring few nutrients. By contrast, cereals such as wholemeal bread, pasta, oats and root vegetables like potatoes and parsnips, bring nourishment along with the same amount of calories. They also provide fiber or roughage.

Fats and oils

In the West we consume a lot of energy as fat and sugar, in processed and fast foods (cakes, biscuits, ice-cream, chips and pies). This can result in heart disease and obesity, illnesses which kill around 2.5 million people each year.

A little fat is essential to keep body tissues healthy, for the manufacture of hormones and to carry the vitamins A, D, E and K. Fats are made up of fatty acids. There are saturated and unsaturated fats, referring to how much hydrogen they contain.

Saturated fats, found mainly in animal products, contain cholesterol. Our bodies need this but can produce what they require. Excess cholesterol can clog arteries, leading to increased risk of heart disease. Saturated fats raise blood cholesterol levels while unsaturated fats – such as olive and sunflower oil – lower them.

WHO advises between 15-30 per cent of total energy intake as fat, with no more than 10 per cent of it in the form of saturated fat. So if your calorie intake is 2,600, and 20 per cent of this comes from fat, that would give 520 calories. Since each gram of fat brings nine calories, this means you should eat about 58 g or two ounces a day. The West's daily average is double that, contributing 1,080 calories before adding those from protein and carbohydrates.

Dairy products are laden with saturated fat, especially hard cheeses, cream and whole milk. Choose low-fat yogurt, cottage or low-fat cheese and skimmed milk that also deliver useful protein. Plant foods rich in fats – avocado pears, nuts and seeds – should be eaten in moderation. Unlike crisps or French fries, however, nuts and seeds do also provide protein, vitamins and a substantial amount of fiber. Pulses, whole grains, vegetables and fruit are low in fat.

Vitamins
These are nutrients that the body cannot produce for itself either at all or in sufficient quantities. Vitamins are essential for growth, cell repair and regulating metabolism (the rate at which the body consumes energy). Green leafy vegetables are a major source of many vitamins and minerals – try to eat them uncooked when you can.

Minerals
These keep the body functioning properly. Calcium, iron, potassium and magnesium are the main minerals; others such as zinc and iodine are known as trace elements and are needed only in tiny amounts. ■

fair trade food

Fairly traded (and organic) products are becoming widely available. If you can't find them where you shop, keep asking. Even giant supermarkets have to listen to their customers. They have huge power over producers; this is part of the problem with 'free' trade. So shopping in smaller stores, or through aid organizations, is a good way to support fair trade. The products cost a little more, because fair trade producers are paid above the cost of production.

The price of almost all food commodities from the South has been falling to below production cost, thus impoverishing farmers while traders and retailers have prospered.

Where to buy?
Fair trade food products are available from alternative outlets, see below.

The International Federation for Alternative Trade (IFAT)
A network of fair trade organizations, many of them Southern producers. They have agreed common objectives:
● To improve the livelihoods of producers ● To promote development opportunities for disadvantaged producers ● To raise consumer awareness ● To set an example of partnership in trade ● To campaign for changes in conventional trade ● To protect human rights.
www.ifat.org

IFAT members who sell some of the food products for the recipes in this book:
Australia
Community Aid Abroad Trading: www.caatrading.org.au
Britain
Traidcraft Exchange: www.traidcraft.co.uk

Canada
Level Ground Trading Ltd:
www.levelground.com
Japan
Global Village Fair Trade
Company: www.globalvillage.
org.jp

New Zealand/Aotearoa
Trade Aid Importers Ltd: www.
tradeaid.org.nz
US
Equal Exchange: www.
equalexchange.com

Fair Trade Labelling Organizations International (FLO)
Most national fair trade labels are now members of FLO. Their common principles include:
• Democratic organization of production • Unrestricted access to free trade unions • No child labor • Decent working conditions • A price that covers the costs of production • Long-term relationships • A social premium to improve conditions • Environmental sustainability

The FLO monitoring program ensures that the trading partners comply with fair trade criteria and that individual producers benefit.

Most national fair trade labels adopt the main elements of a common logo (left).
www.fairtrade.net

Britain
The Fairtrade Foundation:
www.fairtrade.org.uk
Canada
TransFair:
www.web.net/fairtrade
Europe
Max Havelaar:
www.maxhavelaar.nl
TransFair: www.transfair.org
Ireland
Fairtrade Mark Ireland: www.
fair-mark.org
US
TransFair:
www.transfairusa.org
Japan
TransFair:
www.transfair-jp.com

index

173